Beaver Kits

by Ruth Owen

Consultants:
Suzy Gazlay, M.A.
Recipient, Presidential Award
for Excellence in Science Teaching

Leah Birmingham, RVT
Assistant Director
Sandy Pines Wildlife Centre
Napanee, Ontario, Canada

BEARPORT
PUBLISHING

New York, New York

Credits

Cover, © Erwin & Peggy Bauer/Bruce Coleman Photography; 4, © Shutterstock; 5, © Wolfgang Bayer/Bruce Coleman Photography; 7, © All Canada Photos/Superstock; 8–9, © imagebroker.net/Superstock; 10, © Yva Momatiuk & John Eastcott/Minden Pictures/ FLPA; 11, © Rolf Kopfle/Ardea; 12–13, © age fotostock/Superstock; 14–15, © Jen & Des Bartlett/Bruce Coleman Photography; 16, © Michael Quinton/Minden Pictures/FLPA; 17, © Dembinsky Photo Ass./FLPA; 18, © Leonard Rue Enterprises/Animals Animals; 19, © JuniorsBildarchiv/Alamy; 20, © imagebroker.net/Superstock; 21, © Dominique Braud/ Animals Animals; 22T, © Denton Rumsey/Shutterstock; 22C, © Wolfgang Bayer/Bruce Coleman Photography; 22B, © Richard Scalzo/Shutterstock; 23T, © Shutterstock; 23B, © All Canada Photos/Superstock.

Publisher: Kenn Goin
Senior Editor: Lisa Wiseman
Creative Director: Spencer Brinker
Design: Alix Wood
Photo Researcher: Ruby Tuesday Books Ltd

Library of Congress Cataloging-in-Publication Data

Owen, Ruth, 1967–
  Beaver kits / by Ruth Owen.
    p. cm. — (Wild baby animals)
  Includes bibliographical references and index.
  ISBN-13: 978-1-61772-155-7 (library binding)
  ISBN-10: 1-61772-155-7 (library binding)
  1. Beavers—Infancy—Juvenile literature. I. Title.
  QL737.R632O925 2011
  599.37'039—dc22

                            2010044415

For more information, write to Bearport Publishing Company, Inc., 101 Fifth Avenue, Suite 6R, New York, New York 10003. Printed in the United States of America in North Mankato, Minnesota.

122010
10810CGE

10 9 8 7 6 5 4 3 2 1

Contents

Meet some beaver kits

Two baby beavers play on the edge of a pond.

The babies are called **kits**.

The kits live in a home in the pond.

They live with their mother and father.

Beaver home

Pond

4

Mother beaver

Beaver kits

5

What is a beaver?

Beavers are animals that spend most of their time around water.

They are about as big as a medium-size dog.

Adult beaver size

Beavers have thick, **waterproof** fur.

The fur keeps the beaver's skin dry when it is in water.

Thick fur

Where do beavers live?

Beavers live where there are rivers, ponds, and small **lakes**.

The yellow parts of this map show where beavers live around the world.

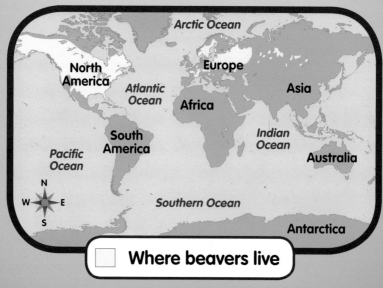

North America

Arctic Ocean

Europe

Atlantic Ocean

Africa

Asia

South America

Indian Ocean

Pacific Ocean

Australia

N
W — E
S

Southern Ocean

Antarctica

Where beavers live

Pond

Beaver builders

Beavers use their long, sharp teeth to cut down trees.

They use the branches from trees to build walls, called **dams**, across rivers.

Branch

Teeth

A dam blocks the flow of river water.

The water backs up behind the dam to make a pond.

The beavers build their home in this pond.

Dam

Pond

Beaver homes

A beaver's home is called a **lodge**.

A lodge is made from sticks and mud.

Lodge

Its entrance is under the water.

Inside the lodge is a cozy room.

This room is above the water.

A Beaver's Lodge

Room

Pond

Entrance

Mothers and kits

In her lodge, a mother beaver gets ready to give birth.

She breaks up sticks and collects grass to make a soft bed for her kits.

After the kits are born, she feeds them milk from her body.

Kit feeding

What do beavers eat?

Beavers eat tree bark and plants.

The kits start to eat bark and plants when they are about two weeks old.

The mother and father bring food to the kits.

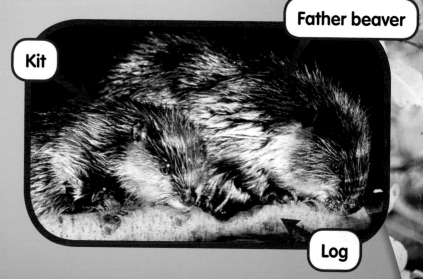

Father beaver

Kit

Log

Time to go outside

The kits first leave the lodge when they are about four weeks old.

They swim in the water near their home.

Their parents show them how to find food.

Soon their parents teach them how to build lodges and dams.

Kit swimming

Mother beaver

Kit

Growing up

The kits stay with their parents for about two years.

During this time, they help build dams and lodges.

They also look after their parents'
new kits.

When they are two years old, they go
off on their own.

It is time to begin their grown-up lives!

Glossary

dams (DAMZ) structures that are built across streams or rivers to stop or slow down the flow of water

kits (KITS) the babies of some animals, such as skunks and beavers

lakes (LAKES) large bodies of water

lodge (LOJ) a home where beavers rest, hide from enemies, and have babies; it's built from sticks and mud

waterproof (WAW-tur-PROOF) able to keep water from passing through

23

Index

Read more

Hall, Margaret. *Beavers.* Mankato, MN: Capstone (2006).

Hodge, Deborah. *Beavers.* Toronto: Kids Can Press (1998).

Kalman, Bobbie. *The Life Cycle of a Beaver.* New York: Crabtree (2007).

Martin-James, Kathleen. *Building Beavers.* Minneapolis, MN: Lerner (2000).

Learn more online

To learn more about beavers, visit **www.bearportpublishing.com/WildBabyAnimals**

About the author

Ruth Owen has been writing children's books for more than ten years. She lives in Cornwall, England, just minutes from the ocean. Ruth loves gardening and caring for her family of llamas.